Patchtown

Life in Eckley Miners' Village
1860 - 1920

Jolene Busher

Cover image: *James Mason* by Robin Spring Bloom

Patchtown: Life in Eckley Miners' Village 1860-1920

FIRST SUNBURY PRESS EDITION

Printed in the United States of America
October 2011

ISBN 978-1-934597-71-2

Published by:
Sunbury Press, Inc.
2200 Market Street
Camp Hill, PA   17011

www.sunburypress.com

Camp Hill, Pennsylvania   USA

In local parlance, a patchtown is a community of coal miners, laborers, skilled workers, community leaders, and their families that would develop around the anthracite coal mining collieries in Northeast Pennsylvania.

Acknowledgments

The author of *Patchtown* would like to thank Eckley Miners' Village, a Pennsylvania Historical and Museum Commission site, for her use of their primary sources and for the opportunity to present the persons that gave Eckley life in the nineteenth and early twentieth centuries.

Table of Contents

Illustrations by Robin Spring Bloom

Introduction

The native Lenape tribes called the land *towamensing*, the wild place, and believed that anyone who would settle in this dense and dark forest, so far from water and on infertile rocky soil, was unfit to live themselves. Local history, or perhaps legend, tells of a pioneer family who was massacred by natives for settling in the outer reaches of towamensing; the natives believed they put the crazed family out of their misery, for why would they dare to settle in a land possessed by evil spirits? The white settlers who would later come to towamensing, or what is now considered Carbon and Luzerne counties, with their maps, surveying tools, and investors were not coming to farm the land as the Lenape believed, but to dig far below the dense woods for something businessmen from Philadelphia and beyond were willing to risk for, despite the warnings of dark spirits lurking above the surface. Still, the Lenapes were not wrong in their forebodings, something dark did dwell deep in towamensing, however, it was something far more valuable than the natives ever imagined. *Black diamonds*, the anthracite coal that was fueling the industrial revolution in the United States, weaved deep through the mountains in thick black veins. After the discovery of this invaluable black rock in towamensing, the surface would begin to reshape itself, first by the anthracite coal companies who would delve with their laborers deep into the earth, but later by the thousands of individuals and families who would settle in a land once damned by the Lenapes, looking for work and a chance at a better life.

Towamensing, once a wild, damned place to the Lenapes, became Saint Anthony's Wilderness to the entrepreneurs, workers, and families who would develop communities and patchtowns around which they worked the land not for agriculture, but for the anthracite coal beneath the surface. In an isolated community in the heart of this wilderness, Shingletown, humble residents manufactured wooden roof slates until industrialists Richard Sharpe, Francis Weiss, and John Leisenring leased the land from the Tench Coxe Estate to mine anthracite coal for the Sharpe, Weiss, and Company. By 1854 extraction of anthracite began, and the Company turned Shingletown into the company-owned town of Eckley, Pennsylvania, which would soon support over one thousand residents of laborers, company employees, skilled craftsmen, clergy, and their families. Even after changing hands when the Sharpe, Weiss, and Company lease was terminated in the 1870's, Eckley, as a company town, continued to mine the rock that made many men rich, and kept many others subjected to continuous debt and at a social deadlock. By the time major anthracite mining productions ended at Eckley's Council Ridge Colliery in the middle of the twentieth century, Eckley could bear witness to the many years of labor and social challenges and victories that took place in anthracite communities all over Northeastern Pennsylvania.

Today along Eckley's Main Street stand the modest homes built by the Sharpe, Weiss, and Company for their workers, and the aged dwellings remain as a skeleton of an anthracite boom town, its residents long lost to history. Memories of Eckley's nineteenth and twentieth century residents were forgotten when mining operations ended, forcing laborers to look elsewhere for work, or as family lines died off, leaving the personal stories of these thousands of individuals to lay in wait quietly behind the walls of the company-built houses. Within each of these homes families, boarders, and friends gathered to share the fears of working within the earth beyond the reach of sunlight, to celebrate the birth of a son, the marriage of a daughter, to mourn the death of a father, and to take part in the labor and social challenges facing an anthracite workforce of immigrants. These struggles and triumphs of Eckley's residents are now mostly unremembered, yet are not lost to historical interpretations and recreations. Even with the loss of the presence and voices from Eckley's past, their memory can always be resurrected by such recreations to once again occupy the homes and walk the streets of their patchtown, an industrial community that rose from the Jurassic wilderness of Northeastern Pennsylvania.

Historical Note
The featured persons appearing in the following vignettes are actual residents who lived in Eckley, Pennsylvania during the decades of 1860, 1870, 1880, 1900, 1910, and 1920. Their names, occupations, and social statuses come from the United States Census Records on file at Eckley Miners' Village, a Pennsylvania Historical & Museum Commission site. The events in the narratives are based on actual events in and around Eckley, Pennsylvania during the nineteenth and twentieth centuries.

1860

By the 1860 census, the Sharpe, Weiss, and Company had been extracting anthracite coal from the Council Ridge Colliery in Eckley, Pennsylvania for a short six years. As a new company apart of the anthracite boom in the 1850's, Sharpe, Weiss, and Company regularly dealt with the business and labor struggles expected in an industry still very young in northeastern Pennsylvania. Market fluctuation, transporting coal from an isolated location in the wilderness, and competition with neighboring and older collieries were continuous business struggles for Richard Sharpe and his company. In addition to fiscal uncertainties, often times the elements and the wilderness around Eckley had the advantages of putting Council Ridge Colliery on top of the market and competition, and just as quickly drop the company on its head. As if the business end of mining at Council Ridge Colliery was not enough to preoccupy the company, labor conflicts were becoming more of a problem even as early as 1860 for the benevolent Richard Sharpe, who worked desperately to keep his workforce employed and contented, as well as make a substantial profit despite the instability of his new company.

Sharpe's workforce was just as dynamic as his business troubles. Men and their families flocked to Eckley from Western Europe and New England, seeking job opportunities in the anthracite boom, and by 1860 Eckley supported a community of just over one thousand residents from England, Ireland, Wales, and a small population of Germans, Hessians, and Scots. The Irish in 1860 were the largest immigrant workforce of mine laborers, with a few skilled workers and a hopeful seven men working as in mine management and as engineers, compared to the English's three engineers and the Welsh's one superintendent. Eckley's second and third generation Pennsylvanians and New Yorkers displayed more variety in their occupations, identifying themselves as boatmen, lock tenders, and farmers who were trading in their jobs on the canals and on the farm for more profitable job opportunities in the mines. Women, too, found occupations in Eckley's fast developing community as domestics and hotel keepers, and men not employed by Sharpe, Weiss, and Company provided services as clergymen, lawyers, butchers, shoemakers, and peddlers.

Just as Eckley and the Council Ridge Colliery were quickly developing into a community and business, the American Civil War broke out in 1861, and defined the divided nation for the next four years. Eckley and its surrounding communities answered Lincoln's call for volunteers, and workers from Eckley traded their picks for rifles to make up companies from Pennsylvania's 81st regiment, which suffered casualties all over the South and in Gettysburg, Pennsylvania, just a few days' journey from their company-rented homes in Eckley. The Civil War affected Eckley as a community and the Council Ridge Colliery as a business, both suffered from the shortages of men in the community and the mines. Richard Sharpe himself supported miners' draft protests in 1863, despite the orneriness of men in the mines who took advantage of the labor shortage to strike and negotiate wages.

By 1869, Sharpe, Weiss, and Company's twenty year contract from the Tench Coxe estate to mine coal at Council Ridge Colliery had only five years left. In the past fifteen years, Eckley's population boomed from a small population of shingle farmers to a diverse anthracite workforce, and the Council Ridge Colliery not only managed to stay on its feet, but to establish itself as a profitable mining operation. The brief episodes of labor conflicts did little to disrupt the company or the community, and Richard Sharpe was able to shelter Eckley from the labor violence beginning to erupt in anthracite fields west and south of the Council

Ridge Colliery. However in 1869, it was unclear whether the benevolent arm Sharpe had stretched around Eckley would survive his departure in the 1870's.

James Mason, Farm Laborer

James Mason lied when he told his foreman that he was born in Pennsylvania. James feared the retributions he, his wife, and his seven children would face should the foreman and his coworkers know where he was truly born, where his parents and sisters still labored, should they even still be alive. In this village James was used to the exclusion and prejudice of his neighbors and coworkers. Social rejection was expected for James and his family, and while it was an uncomfortable life, it was much more preferable to the life James was born into. James was a quiet man in the mines, though he often told his children tall tales and laughed heartily at the trouble his toddlers Joseph and John managed to get into. Yet in the mines, James was nearly silent. He feared if he spoke the men would recognize his drawl, and they would figure out that James was born in the South, he worried they would tell the foreman that he was born in South Carolina, that he was born a slave.

James' wife Lucy and all his children were born free in Lancaster, Pennsylvania, but they all feared the day James' status as an escaped slave would be discovered, and the whole family could find themselves in chains, laboring, sweating, and bleeding in the cotton fields of South Carolina. Living in this constant fear kept James silent in the coal mines, where his rectitude stopped any real attempts to form any friendships, should the other laborers break their prejudices to even joke with James. Despite this, James found comfort in the depths of the earth where he labored - while his coworkers cursed the dark damp James sought refuge, the cool darkness a favorable exchange for dry, sweltering cotton fields.

James had not always worked in the mines alongside Irishmen and Englishmen. Two years earlier, incapable of managing his own farm, James moved his family from Lancaster to the northern anthracite fields seeking better sources of income. Rejected from employment in mines near Pottsville and Summit Hill, James' wagon, filled with his family, farm tools he could never use, and twenty-five dollars of personal estate, traveled slowly up the mountain road towards the Council Ridge Colliery and the accompanying Eckley village in Pennsylvania. Having no experience working deep in the earth, but not a stranger to hard labor, James worked as a laborer in the mines twelve hours a day, six days a week, for six months a year alongside men from Ireland, England, Wales, and other parts of the United States, all with their own hesitations towards the silent darkie in the mines. To the Irish, James was a threat, to the English and Welsh, a bumbling fool.

Despite their preconceptions, James was not a man bothered by their crude remarks and mistreatment, but he was a man who delighted in tales of irony and surprise endings. While he kept quiet at work in the mines along the Irishmen and Welshmen who laughed at his black skin, James laughed to himself. It was true, that in the morning the Irishman, the Welshman, the Englishman and James entered the mine as obviously different men, but at the end of the day they all emerged as hard worked, tired laborers. They emerged as the same - laborers with black faces.

James McLelens, Superintendent of the Mines

Winter in Eckley was a difficult time of year for James McLelens. In January the winter winds blew down Main Street, mixing the falling snow with the settled coal dust, creating an apparition of a divine battle of angels and demons as the white snow and black coal dust violently tangled with each other in the wind. Once the mines closed for the season, James

spent most of his time inside his single home in the west end of the village, and despite the company of his parents, sister, and five children, James felt very bitter and alone. In the winter months James lost the camaraderie of the other men in the mines, each worker boarded up in his rented home, venturing out only to collect firewood or hunt local game. Inside his own home, the children grew restless, as did the hostility of his father as the grey months dragged on. Like every other spring, James knew that even when the mines opened again his father's attitudes would remain the same, but at least when they entered the mines in the morning they could go their separate ways, allowing James a twelve-hour escape from the resentment he had grown accustomed to.

Seven years earlier when James and his father brought their family to Eckley, both James and his father entered the mines as inexperienced laborers. While James Sr. continued to work the same position everyday, back bent in a monkey vein, ankles deep in water, James Jr.'s skills advanced and were wasted on menial labor. James quickly became a favorite of his superiors, becoming a certified miner within three years, a foreman in just one more, and finally a superintendent after spending five years below the earth's surface at the Council Ridge Colliery. James' progress afforded his family a single home, in exchange for the cramped half double they rented in the east end of the village, but it could not pay for his father's gratitude. James' father remained the symbolic head of the household, but as an unskilled laborer he could not give his family half the salary that his son earned as a superintendent.

A father's resentment of his sons was an inherited quality of the McLelens family and one of the few family treasures brought over from Ireland. Rather than feeling gratitude or pride of his son's success in the mines, James Sr. felt that his patriarchy was threatened, and his resentment festered over time, making life miserable in the family's single home. Crowded together in the wintertime, James' relationship with his father became even more suffocating, but it was not only his father's hostility that made James lonely this time of year. On the January night James' youngest son William was born, the exhausted screams of James' wife were silenced by the howling of the wind outside as she died bringing into the world the son James would resent, resent even more than his own father resented his authority in the mines, the son who would not be able to escape his own snarls and stares, because resentment of sons was an inherited quality of the McLelens family.

Richard Sharpe, Mine Owner

When Richard Sharpe received his post early in the morning, he was not surprised to see the rushed script of Ario Pardee the Senior, his competitor and former ally as a Lehigh regional coal operator. Richard sat back in his parlor and laughed to himself as he read Pardee's accusations of Sharpe's loyalty and he was amused to imagine Pardee writing this letter to him in a fit of rage and bewilderment. Pardee's letter spat at Richard for being a benevolent fool and an ignorant operator, and concluded with instructions that Richard return to England to resume his former occupation as a farmer, that he was better suited for managing pigs and manure than men and profit. Perhaps Pardee's accusations were correct, however Richard did not feel that inciting a strike with his own workforce as honorable means to raise profits, or to maintain a healthy relationship with his workers. As an allied coal operator, Pardee expected Richard to lower his worker's wages, forcing them to strike, which would strategically increase consumer demand for coal and bring Sharpe, Pardee, and other operators one last sizeable profit before the mines closed within a month. To Richard, this was corruption in its purest form, and not at all how he felt a respectable business should conduct itself. No, Richard's alliance was not to operators like Pardee who cheated his workers. His alliance was to the men who labored for him, and who he believed were at the mercy of his decisions.

Richard remembered what it was like to physically labor to earn a living, he did not always make profits based on business deals made in a hotel parlor far away from the colliery. As a young man he worked a farm in America's wilderness, and only through chance meetings and smart deals became a mine merchant at Council Ridge Colliery, living in the gothic white house in the west end of the village. Unlike most mine merchants in nearby collieries, Richard sympathized with his workers, he understood their worries when the coal market slumped and their wages dropped. As a businessman Richard knew that to keep laborers from leaving to work for the competition, you must lower your prices to increase their wages at the sacrifice of profit. But as a former laborer himself, Richard would rather suffer some profit loss than force his workers to struggle to keep the potatoes, bread, and butter on their tables. When market demands for coal were low, or when Council Ridge Colliery struggled to compete with neighboring collieries, Richard employed his mine laborers to build roads around the village, when he could not pay them to mine coal. During the War when Lincoln's draft threatened to take away unwilling miners, Richard intervened with local recruiting officers to spare his community of workers, and when the Draft was protested, he personally hammered a notice on the blacksmith's shop warning his workers not to bother coming to work, since draft protests would take place the next day in Hazleton, and their labors were more necessary there. For Richard, the Draft had not been a matter of losing his workforce. On the contrary, he would have profited by sending his miners to the War and hiring new workers at much lower wages. The Draft had threatened the welfare of his community, and rather than take advantage of its salary slashing opportunities, Richard attacked it with vehemence.

However recently, despite his continuous efforts to keep his community employed and contented, Richard realized that he could not keep every worker happy. It was difficult to compete with neighboring collieries who temporarily offered higher wages, or with the violent fervor of new labor unions. More alarmingly, the Lehigh region coal merchants' recent move to force their laborers to strike was a prelude to the games companies were willing to play with their workers, and Richard was unwilling to become a player. He wanted to pay them what his profits would allow, and continue to offer opportunities to his community to compensate for slow markets. Richard did not want to strategize strikes and negotiate alliances with other collieries. He wanted to maintain a direct relationship with every worker at his mines as he had in the past, but such relationships were becoming more complicated and strained, despite Richard's benevolence in the past.

Richard was beginning to think that despite Pardee's cruel accusations, perhaps he was better suited for managing pigs than men. Richard's mines were becoming a part of a larger network of collieries, miners, and labor struggles that he could no longer imagine to control. Negotiating grievances with his workers would be more difficult when they no longer represented just themselves but a larger union, and he could only build so many more roads to compensate for slow markets before his workers would strike or leave Eckley all together. In a few more years, his company's lease with the Coxe estate would expire, and rather than renew his contract, Richard was contemplating retirement. Richard was beginning to see the types of bloody games collieries were willing to play with their workers and communities, and he did not want to be a part of this new social struggle. Perhaps he was getting too old, or perhaps he just did not have the malice in him required to operate his colliery the way other merchants like Ario Pardee Sr. expected him to. For the time being, Richard could only continue to protect his colliery and community from the approaching social storm, but he could not stay to endure it, in a few years Richard would leave Eckley indefinitely.

1870

In 1874 the twenty year contract between the Sharpe, Weiss, and Company and the Tench Coxe estate had expired and the company disbanded, though mining at the Council Ridge Colliery was resumed by Eckley B. Coxe, the grandson of Tench Coxe. While some operators from the former Sharpe, Weiss, and Company would stay on to work at Council Ridge Colliery with Eckley B. Coxe, such as John Leisenring, Richard Sharpe and other operators of the original company retired and left Eckley, Pennsylvania, never to return. The mines operated as they had for the past twenty years, though miners and laborers in 1874 might have wondered what the transition in business and community leadership could mean for their livelihoods after they had grown comfortable with, and appreciative of, Richard Sharpe.

The demographics in Eckley had changed very little from the previous census in 1860, though the English and Welsh populations were surpassed by the influx of Germans to Eckley, who worked in the mines and as skilled craftsmen in the village. The Irish continued to make up the majority of the workforce in the mines, both as certified miners and laborers, and they maintained miscellaneous occupations in the community. Second and third generation Pennsylvanians continued to add variety to Eckley's community with more skilled craftsmen, as well as a shoemaker and a dress maker, who added fashionable class to the industrial community.

If the Civil War defined American history in the 1860's, the anthracite fields of Pennsylvania were defined by the Molly Maguires in the 1870's. Soon after the Civil War ended in 1865, the Irish who worked menial positions in the Pennsylvania anthracite mines for little pay and at great personal risk began to unite behind some of the area's first labor unions to voice grievances and negotiate better wages and safer working conditions in the mines. Often, rebellious Irish laborers and miners grew impatient between the social and class struggles with their White Anglo Saxon and Protestant mine superiors, and violent confrontations resulted in the destruction of homes and personal property of particularly malicious mine owners and supervisors. Often times in these outbursts of violence, labor and social oppressors were physically assaulted or in some instances, killed.

Anthracite communities in the 1870's feared the advent of strikes, not only because a strike could mean days, weeks, or months without pay in an already unstable industry, but patchtowns and larger communities fearfully anticipated the eruption of violence that often accompanied strikes and other labor disputes. Violent attacks on colliery owners and supervisors were eventually blamed on the supposed secret society of Irish miners and laborers, infamously remembered as the Molly Maguires. Whether this group of labor vigilantes or dynamite terrorists existed or not, the Catholic Church was pressured to control their congregations of angry Irish miners, so men suspected of memberships to any secret society, mainly to the Molly Maguires, were threatened with excommunication – the Catholic sentence worst than death. Eventually in 1877 the first of some twenty Irishmen were convicted and executed as Molly Maguires by the State of Pennsylvania. The trial was a victory for the prosecution led by Franklin B. Gowen, president of the Philadelphia and Reading Railroad, and personal lawyer of Eckley B. Coxe, then operator of Coxe Bros. & Co. of the mines in Eckley and other neighboring patchtowns, which were overwhelmingly manned by an Irish workforce.

Despite the business connection between Eckley B. Coxe and the leading prosecutor of the Molly Maguires, the community in Eckley suffered from very little labor violence during the 1870's, though communities very nearby, such as Summit Hill and Tamaqua, did. Coxe's home near Eckley in Drifton was never attacked by angry laborers, and Mrs. Sophia Coxe, Eckley's wife, contrasted the emotionally displaced mine owners targeted by violent labor attacks as a benevolent woman interested in the well-being of her husband's mining communities.

Michael Fallihee, Catholic Priest

Father Michael Fallihee rearranged the altar after Good Friday services, and a cloud of incense lingered like ghostly apparitions in pews of the Church of the Immaculate Conception in Eckley, with only the rays from the sun splintering through the smoke. The parishioners had returned to their homes to continue their fasting, and Father Fallihee wondered if his message for this Good Friday, sacrifice and faith, had the effect he intended on his congregation – particularly with the laborers at the Council Ridge Colliery.

Father Fallihee could not understand why so many men, Christian men, would burrow into the earth where the brightness of the sun and the warmth of life could not be felt. Good Christian men should live their lives striving to become closer to God, not digging their way closer to Hell, and the Evil One. Christ spent three days in Hell so that Christian men would not have to, yet what was the value of these black diamonds – was their price so high that men were so willing to send other men into the treacheries of Hell, putting them at risk of physical danger and mortal destruction? Apparently so, with the demand of anthracite so high in America, the demands of Father's congregation were even higher. Father Fallihee was not an ignorant man. He knew men had to work to eat, work to care for their families, and work to live - his own parents had escaped famine in Ireland to find work in America. Sympathetic, Father could not fault the men in his congregation for working in the mines. The men had relatively steady employment and at the Council Ridge Colliery, a decent wage – yet was working in the mines worth the dangerous risk of their lives, and now, even their souls?

Since before the Civil War, trouble had been brewing in the anthracite fields west and south of Eckley, and Father Fallihee worried that it was only a matter of time before it reached this isolated patchtown. Unlike Irish laborers in these other fields, Irish workers at Eckley had opportunities in the past to negotiate grievances personally with Richard Sharpe, but now he was gone, and at times the men grew restless. The Diocese warned Father of approving the men in his congregation to join fraternal orders, the secret societies that were now at the center of the labor struggle in anthracite Pennsylvania. Whereas in the past Father Fallihee had encouraged such memberships – membership benefits extended to the tables and pantries of widows – he now had to take a determined opposition against them ever since the Diocese threatened excommunication to suspected members, a punishment encouraged by railroad and mining companies. Men, their souls so weak to the temptations of the Evil One, were now not only willing to deny men safe working conditions and fair wages, but also deny them their souls.

Father knew Irishmen fighting for unionization and social change were left with few options to turn to, other than themselves, other than even violence, but Father Fallihee also knew the position of the Diocese - membership and activity in such orders earned a sentence of excommunication, a signing over of a ones soul to the Evil One. The very best Father could do, was preach peace and faith in Christ, and warn his flock that violence in the anthracite fields would only lead to further opposition, so let the miners and laborers practice peace for unionization. Was this not what Christ had done? Did he not practice peace? Christ's earthly sacrifice granted heaven for the souls waiting to enter the gates, and Father truly believed that with peace and persistence, his workers would be victorious, and could save their souls. Still, Father Fallihee was not a foolish man. He knew that even with peace, victory would not come without great sacrifice from his congregation – but he hoped to present Jesus Christ as the greatest example of what a man's self-sacrifice could accomplish.

Peter Russell, Episcopal Minister

Reverend Peter Russell enjoyed the two hour ride back to Eckley from his other congregation in White Haven, at St. Paul's. The short journey gave him time alone with his thoughts, and as of late, Reverend Russell had very little time to himself. Reverend Russell especially enjoyed the company of his mount, the old and humble brown gelding he bought from an Irish widow in Eckley's east end, more so because he knew the woman needed the fifteen dollars the old horse was not worth. The gelding at least did not complain, as the Reverend's parish did, that his singing was off key, and he did not intrude on the quiet solitude Reverend Russell looked so forward to on Sunday afternoons.

The ride on the twisting mountain roads took the Reverend through dense woods, still undisturbed by the Lehigh Valley Railroad's lines and mining collieries. In these woods the senses could be cleansed of the industrial smells, noises, and eyesores that filled the nostrils and ears, and saddened the eyes in Eckley. The monstrous breakers and pillars of coal dust that darkened the sky were replaced by towering trees, old enough to remember the frightened footfalls of the Lenape who had rarely ventured under their canopies.

On this ride the Reverend's ears were also filled with the sounds of birds calling to each other and the rustle of underbrush as game ran from the sound of the gelding's hoof steps. He preferred these sweet noises to the breaker whistle that blasted at scheduled intervals throughout the day, and the continuous rattling, drumming, and snorting from the colliery. In the winter these woods were white, ashen brown, and evergreen, in the spring budding-yellow, in the summer luscious green, and in autumn the forest was ablaze in bright reds, rusted browns, and smoldering oranges. Much differently, in the village of Eckley, no matter the season a thick layer of black coated the trees, the homes and churches, the gardens, the laundry hanging on the line, everything – the dust was indiscriminate in its falling. The most disturbing sight, however, were the persons Reverend Russell saw, particularly in the east end of Eckley where the poorest laborers and families rented their company homes.

Though the majority of his congregation resided in the west end of Eckley, Reverend Russell often visited families, widows, and disabled workers in the east end of Eckley, the Catholic neighborhood. Despite their difference in denomination and histories, the Reverend enjoyed the company of the Catholic Pastor, and they both agreed that their friendship was important in maintaining a benign relationship between the east and west ends of Eckley. In the industrial and social storm between English and Irish, management and laborers, the rich and poor in neighboring anthracite communities, Reverend Russell wanted Eckley's predominately lower class work force to know that his congregation was not their cultural enemy, and in his sermons he reminded his parish of Christ's teachings on charity, agape.

Eckley was not a very big village, the east end was not a far walk from the west end, and exchanges between the classes and denominations could not be avoided. In an attempt to encourage happy relationships between the two ends of the village, Reverend Russell's favorite lesson to foul-mouthed adolescent boys in his congregation was to assign them the duty of chopping firewood for widows in the east end. The boys, forgiven for their misbehaviors, usually continued to collect firewood for widows and elderly workers long after their lessons were learned. And truly, Reverend Russell could seldom remember any real displays of religious or social animosities. He also liked to believe this was a result of the efforts he made in creating community between the two ends of the village.

This was not to say that there weren't lower class workers who resented their neighbors in the west end, or members in his congregation who did not feel they owed charities to their neighbors in the east end, but such feelings were hardly expressed despite the social anxieties that existed in the heredities of the rich and poor, the English and Irish, Catholicism and the Church of England. Yet, even as the brown gelding bumped down the winding mountain road towards Eckley, Reverend Russell questioned his own social anxieties and motives for communal peace in his parish's patchtown. As an Episcopal minister, the Reverend had certain obligations to the Church and to his parish, and as an Englishman he had certain obligations to fulfill socially. It might not be in the Reverend's best interests to mingle with a Catholic Priest, give charities to an Irish community, and lecture his parish on the importance of communal peace with Catholics. With years of social unrest and religious fury behind him, why did the Reverend bother to break social and religious barriers in Eckley? Did he truly wish to see a non-prejudiced relationship between the two Churches, the two ethnic groups, the two classes? Was this a realistic goal, and was this a goal he not only encouraged, but prayed for? The Reverend's social and religious obligations told him no, communal peace between the classes and Churches in Eckley was not only unattainable, but undesirable.

And already there it was, the Reverend's tongue tasted it and his nostrils tickled with it before Eckley even came into view. Coal dust and earthy fumes from the Council Ridge Colliery smoked the air even on a Sunday. Even on the Lord's Day of Rest, the lower class Irish laborers of Eckley choked on it, the skilled Germans and the English in the west end shook it from their clothes and rubbed it out of their eyes. *Thou shall keep holy the Sabbath –* but what was so holy about the Day of Rest when the senses were constantly reminded of the troubles that waited the next morning in the dark of the mines and in the widow's kitchens? Making his way down Main Street, past the Church of the Immaculate Conception, past the shanties of the Irish laborers and slate pickers, past the shoeless children darting in front of his gelding, past the old men missing their legs and the young men missing their hands, past the darting eyes of young widows, and past the dirty, skinny, and staring young orphans, Reverend Russell's humanity clutched at his throat.

In front of him and behind him, coal dust fell like snow painted black in mourning, and the Reverend knew if the Irish Catholic laborers in the east end were not working the lower paid and more dangerous positions in the mines, his English congregation would be. The mines were indiscriminate to whose husband it traps and suffocates, white damp was indiscriminate to whose son it chokes to death, just as the coal dust was indiscriminate to where it fell. Only society discriminates, when the mines would just as quickly kill Eckley B. Coxe as it would his poorest employee. If the earth struck without prejudice, who was the Reverend to discriminate men because of their race, religion, or social status? And yet he already knew, that despite his social and religious obligations, Reverend Russell could not discriminate, and he did willingly pray for communal peace in this patchtown with real intention. How could he deny the larger half of Eckley's community the charities and personhoods he granted parish? He could not, and just as the mines were indiscriminate to the households they brought grief and tragedy to, Reverend Russell was indiscriminate to the men and women he prayed for, and the men and women he gave personhood.

The brown gelding stopped in front of the Reverend's company-rented home before he even realized they had entered the west end of Eckley. Turning in his saddle, Reverend Russell looked back towards the east end, enveloped in coal dust. He knew that for this patchtown to survive, the market for coal had to remain profitable to employ the laborers, the miners, the skilled craftsmen, and the parish that funded his own salary. But for this *community* to survive, the patchwork of lower and upper class laborers, Irish, English, Germans, and Catholics, Episcopalians and Presbyterians, their charities and good will to one another needed to fall as indiscriminately as the coal dust on their rooftops. Reverend Russell dismounted the gelding, and in his flat key of C sang,

> *We gather together to ask the Lord's blessing,*
> *He chastens and hastens His will to make known,*
> *The wicked oppressing now cease from distressing,*
> *Sing praises to His Name; He forgets not His own!*

1880

The 1880 census left behind the violent turbulence of the Molly Maguires and the 1870's, but for patchtowns in anthracite Pennsylvania, working in the mines and living in company-owned communities did not change for the better just because the Molly Maguire trials and executions ended in the late 1870's. The prosecutors in the Molly Maguire trials were successful in destroying early attempts at unionization, which would have given miners a much needed venue for voicing grievances and negotiating wages. Miners and laborers were still striking for higher wages and better working conditions, but too often mine operators would hire scabs willing to accept cheaper wages, or temporarily use the strike to raise market demand for anthracite, adding more profits to their personal bank accounts.

The workforce at the Council Ridge Colliery was still dominated by Western Europeans, largely German and Irish laborers and skilled craftsmen. With a population still just above one thousand, Eckley's community was beginning to decline, very slightly, in comparison to the previous decades in the census records of the village. Still, Eckley continued to function as a typical late nineteenth century working community, now providing schooling for ninety eight children, mostly second and third generation Pennsylvanians.

Working conditions in the mines were still dangerous and not strictly regulated by safety standards, as reflected in Eckley's 1880 census records, which reveals a high number of men listed as maimed, blind, crippled, or unemployed - results from work related accidents in the mines. In Eckley and other patchtowns belonging to Coxe Bros. & Co.'s collieries, however, Mrs. Sophia Coxe personally delivered medicines and other medical supplies to the ill, injured and disabled to ease some of the burden of struggling families, because an injured man was an unemployed man, and an unemployed laborer could not provide for his family in a company-owned patchtown.

Catherine Given, Domestic

Catherine Given learned how to survive on a coffin ship bound for America when she was ten years old. When the crops failed in 1868, Catherine's father's health also began to fail, and on a night in October her father collapsed to the floor never to rise again. Losing her husband and her financial stability, Catherine's mother Mary made the decision to leave for America with her daughter to live with her brother's family in New York City. However for Mary Given, their ship would not take her to America, because only three days into their voyage, Mary contracted severe coughs, shakes, and delirium. Continually forcing Catherine away from her, Mary Given coughed blood into her chemise for four nights until Catherine found her pale and stiff on the cramped floor in the lower deck of the Bark Britannia. That morning following a very informal service, Catherine watched as her mother was thrown overboard into the Atlantic, along with five other passengers, to join her husband in the hereafter. Catherine, ten years old, was alone.

When her ship made port in New York City, Catherine succumbed to the human fear of loneliness, and followed the crowd leaving the Bark Britannia to a train station that would take them to Wilkes Barre, Pennsylvania. Both on board the ship and there on the train Catherine heard talk of work in the anthracite fields, and with the prospect of work, she followed the hungry crowd of men from New York to Wilkes Barre, Pennsylvania, and finally to a dirty settlement of red houses identified as Eckley, Pennsylvania by a coal dust covered post

near the entrance of the village. Again following the crowd, this time of women, Catherine found herself at the end of the village in front of a large white house, blossoming with flora along the porch. Falling in with the uniformed domestics, Catherine became employed cleaning the delicate china and crystal of Sally Sharpe, her tiny fingers worked more carefully than the fat clumsy fingers of Cat Parry, a Welsh domestic with a bitter tongue.

Over the years Catherine grew used to Cat the sour spinster, and also learned to love her independence - her income and well-being was determined only by how well she washed sheets and dressed the Sharpe children, and later the Leisenring children. As a single woman and a domestic in the Sharpe home, Catherine did not worry what would happen to her if crops failed or if a husband would become disabled or die in the mines. This is why when the handsome Irishman John Kane gave Catherine promises of matrimony, she refused him. Catherine had learned that stability was survival, and the instability of becoming a coal miner's wife meant being subjected to the uncertainty of income and survival in Eckley. Catherine was content to grow old and remain unwedded as Cat Parry had done, caring for the Sharpe home and its continually changing residents. Even though she dreamed of hearing happy voices of the children she would never have and the companionship of a husband, Catherine was satisfied in knowing she would never be thrown overboard a ship to decay at the bottom of the ocean.

C.M. Howell and Alfred McCollum, Clerks in Company Store

Every Friday evening when Peggy Boyle came into the company store, she made her way to the back of the store where the week old produce, poorer cuts of meat, and flour sprinkled with tiny worms sitting in mice bitten sacks waited in neglect, the better meats and grains already picked over throughout the week. Peggy was not disgusted by the small green patches on the pig's head or the brown spots on the soft apples, and she did not mind the inconvenience of sifting out the tiny worms and mice droppings from her flour before making a week's supply of bread. Peggy was grateful enough to at least have this meager selection – by the age of sixty-eight she and her husband John had already done without even this. Gathering what leftover, nearly spoiled goods she believed she could afford, Peggy limped to the front of the store, and arranged her items on the counter with such gentle anticipation, that anyone would think she was placing delicate crystal on an uneven shelf. Peggy always made sure to shop at the company store on Friday evenings before closing, because she was sure to be waited on by Charles Howell or his brother Alfred McCollum, and neither of these clerks bothered her about her husband's outstanding tab. In fact, Charles and Alfred had not added anything to John Boyle's tab in the last ten years, but out of respect of the old man, when Peggy asked for her purchase to be put on their tab, Charles or Alfred scribbled on a scrap, mock tab, that they would crumble as soon as Peggy slowly made her way down to the east end of Eckley.
Neither Charles nor Alfred ever worked in the mines at Eckley, but that did not mean that they were unfamiliar with the hardships that often afflicted families whose provider had risked the dangers of laboring deep within the earth, and consequently lost the ability to pay their rent, purchase their flour, and call on the company doctor. Working together in the company store, Charles and Alfred had seen men seeking employment in the mines, but too poor to pay for their equipment, wives selling eggs to pay off their husband's tab, but still without enough money to pay for flour, and young girls picking out material to sew clothing for wealthier clients, but dressed themselves in dresses too short and shoes too thin. Charles would remark to Alfred that the welfare of the people is best reflected in their tabs and purchases at the

Jolene Busher

18

company store, and while conditions in Eckley were better in comparison to other mining towns, the village was not without impoverished households.

John Boyle's circumstance was one of the most pitiful Charles and Alfred had seen working for the Council Ridge Colliery's company store – Boyle was a seventy year old man who picked slate for the past ten years since he lost both his legs and two sons in the mines. Realistically, John and Peggy had no options. John was too old and disabled to learn a new trade, and both were too feeble to move away from Eckley. John and Peggy Boyle would stay in Eckley in a slate picker's shack until they died, and judging by the previous winter, neither would be in Eckley, or in this world, much longer. Both Charles and Alfred felt guilty letting Peggy walk out of the store every Friday with rotten goods, but these were the only items that could go missing in inventory without any notice, as long as they were counted as unsold and thrown out goods. So when the brother clerks went home to be fed and fussed by their mother, wives, and sisters, Charles and Alfred wondered what type of meal Peggy could be preparing with pig's feet and old flour as they enjoyed hearty stew and tart pies. And as the wind rattled the thin walls of the slate picker's shack far down the street, chilling the aged bones of Peggy Boyle as she sifted through the old flour from the company store, Charles and Alfred were unable to see how grateful the old woman was to find a few gold coins hiding in the flour sack, and that night Peggy said her prayers of thanksgiving for Charles Howell and Alfred McCollum.

Abraham Peter, Miner

In Germany Abraham Peter's father made clocks, and as a boy he would sit at his father's work bench and watch his father place together the gears and springs with great precision. His father's workshop had always been cluttered with clock faces, carved wooden pinecones, little rooftops, and cuckoos that were all blanketed with a light layer of woodchips leftover from the clock master's late night whittling. The smell of freshly cut wood and the continuous *tick tick tick* of scores of clocks in his father's shop engaged Abraham's senses as a boy and he was sure that when he was old enough, and skilled enough, he would build beautiful clocks as his father had done, and his grandfather had done. His first lessons at constructing a clock were always unsuccessful, but his father laughed and assured him that the cuckoo did not coo because his clock was just made of bad parts, worn out parts, all of which were replaceable. Abraham's father would tussle his hair and his laughter synchronized with the *tick tick tick* of efficiently working clocks, as he tossed broken parts in a pile on the floor. Now, aged fifty-one years old and a miner in the wilderness of Pennsylvania, Abraham felt like the pieces in the junk pile on his father's workshop floor – a worn out and replaceable part.

As a young man Abraham unwillingly left his father's clock shop in Germany to immigrate to America, working on one job to the next, trying to find steady employment. Eventually he found his way to the mines in Eckley, Pennsylvania, where Abraham worked for years as a common laborer until he was skilled enough to pass his certification, and worked as a respectable and accomplished miner at the Council Ridge Colliery. Beginning a new family business tradition, Abraham's son Frederick, named after his grandfather the clock master, would never whittle a cuckoo or arrange gears inside a clock, but would enter the mines at a young age, working as a nipper boy opening and closing the mine doors for twelve hours in the lonely, cold dark of the mines.

Even into his late forties, Abraham entered the mines to work, sitting in the wooden car as it was lowered into the dark, the *tick tick tick* of the track recalling to Abraham his father's clocks. Like a clock on his father's work bench, the whole mine sounded with the *tick tick tick* as all the other working parts picked at the mine walls, the *crunch* as earth was

19

shoveled into coal cars, the *whoosh* as air and debris blasted down the mine shaft - *tick tick tick, crunch, tick tick tick, crunch, whoosh, tick tick tick, crunch*! This mechanism is how Abraham worked in the mines for over twenty years, but like the old parts on the floor of his father's clock shop, Abraham too became defective with time and use, and after the accident that left his legs crippled, Abraham was discarded and replaced by younger and more abler men, newer parts. The years of hard labor Abraham spent in the mines allowed him no compensations, since he was merely a replaceable part that was now broken and useless.

Solely dependent on the salary of his children, Abraham would spend his time on a rocking chair, rocking back and forth as the floor creaked beneath this weight. The slow *tick tick tick* that resonated in the small bedroom came from an old cuckoo clock hanging on the wall, slowing with each swing of the pendulum. Finally when the *tick tick tick* nearly slowed to a stop, Abraham did not rise to push the pendulum back into motion – Abraham closed his eyes, and there was silence.

.

1900

A ten year absence of the census records silenced the dramatic events which occurred in the anthracite coal fields of northeastern Pennsylvania from the 1890's through the 1900's. In 1889 the census doors were slammed shut on the Western Europeans and their early struggles in the coal fields, and when the census doors were opened again in 1900 after remaining closed for too long, suffocated communities of Eastern European workforces were pushing and shoving for air and to escape the gunfire and terror that rained upon them in the decade neglected by the census records. The 1890's introduced Eastern Europeans to anthracite communities in Pennsylvania, and in many patchtowns the demographics changed dramatically. Eastern Europeans quickly replaced the Western Europeans as scabs or as German and Irish laborers moved into higher paid positions in the mines or left the patchtowns altogether.

Eckley's population rose in 1900's census records, still over one thousand, but now closer to twelve hundred. New immigrants from Germany and Ireland accounted for just over one hundred residents, with second and third generation Pennsylvanians with Irish and German descent making up most of the Irish and German communities in Eckley. In 1900's Eckley, however, most of the new immigrants were Eastern Europeans, as was the case in hundreds of other anthracite communities. By 1900 Eckley was introduced to Austrians, Hungarians, Italians, and Poles, who now made up the majority of the workforce in the mines at Council Ridge Colliery. Because of language barriers and work inexperience, most of the new immigrant workers to Eckley worked in the mines as laborers, the 'butty' that worked under the supervision of the contracted certified miners at the Council Ridge Colliery.

If early pushes for unionization and better conditions in the mines during the 1870's and 1880's were an uphill struggle for the Irish and other Western Europeans, the struggles were the same for the new immigrant workforce, but now these men were also trying, and often failing, to push a boulder up the same mountain. In the eyes of Western Europeans and Anglican mine owners, the Eastern Europeans who spoke dozens of bizarre sounding languages, and dressed differently, were regarded as socially strange and backwards. As a consequence of this bigotry, these new miners, laborers, and their families violently encountered prejudices even the Irish never dealt with. But like the oppressed Irish in the coal mines, the Eastern European miners attempted to show their defiance to the unchecked safety conditions and low wages in the mines, though in ways much more humbly than their predecessors had demonstrated.

In 1897 at mines outside of Hazleton, Pennsylvania, Polish, Slavic, and other Eastern Europeans marched from colliery to colliery, encouraging miners to strike for higher wages and safer working conditions in the mines. These unarmed miners and laborers were stopped near mines in Lattimer by local law enforcement, who were giddy for a violent confrontation, but were disappointed to see the marchers armed only with the American flag. When Sheriff Martin took the American flag from its bearer, a confused scuffle began, and the Sheriff's deputies opened fire on the marchers, shooting them where they stood and shooting them in the back as they fled. Nineteen miners were killed in the Lattimer Massacre, but what was really massacred were their new pushes for unionization, and their hopes of improving their lives and the futures of their children.

If 1897 had been a nightmare, the Great Strike of 1902 was a miner's second chance at victory for unionization and fair treatment in the mines. John Mitchell, the young president of the United Mine Workers union led coal communities all over northeastern Pennsylvania on a

163 day strike, forcing the federal government to intervene on behalf of labor. When the Strike of 1902 ended in October of that year, the United Mine Workers union was able to secure, in some cases, a twenty-percent wage increase, a shorter work day, and employee arbitration rights, giving miners the legal opportunity to negotiate wages and settle labor disputes directly with their employers. Despite the months without pay, the meager meals, and risks of being black listed, the laborers a part of the United Mine Workers were able to celebrate a monumental victory in labor history, and looked forward to having more control of their own lives and working conditions.

John Nogal, Mine Laborer

September was a bustling month every year in Eckley, with the mines fixing to be closed for the season in a few short weeks. Families were busy preparing for the long months of winter and their homes were alive with activity. Wives canned the vegetables and fruits they harvested earlier in the month, and husbands disassembled the stove in the summer kitchen to bring back inside the house to keep the family warm throughout the winter months. Children were busy too, little boys and girls picked the last of the berries found in the woods, while their older brothers hunted deer to smoke for the winter and their older sisters mended long underwear. Mimicking the black bear that lived in the woods surrounding Eckley, families patched up the drafts in the homes they rented to make a cozy den for winter while neighbors and coworkers met in kitchens after work, some of their last gatherings before they hid in their homes from bitter cold and chilling winds.

As the rest of the village buzzed with activity and excitement in September, John Nogal and his family could not help but become emotionally removed from their neighbors. John and his wife Augusta, five children, and his very elderly mother, only recently came to Eckley, when John quit his job as a laborer in Pardee's mines near Hazleton in 1897. John's decision to resign was absolute, for while he accepted the dangerous jobs he was given in the mines because of his ignorance, there were other injustices he could not accept.

Living outside the Pardee mine had been comfortable for John and his family. They were neighbors to extended family and other Poles, and spoke Polish in their kitchens and smoke houses. When they left their little community to walk to the company store and other shops however, they were greeted with rocks and racial slurs by their Anglican neighbors. Despite the work conditions in the mines and the social anxieties, John and his coworkers had few options – they had to work in these mines and live in this community or they would starve their families, there was no help from the outside communities, but only the will of laborers like John to take care of their families. For John, his daily encounter with danger both inside and outside the mines had become routine, and quitting his job was still not an option – at least not until September 1897. After that September, John knew that even quitting his dangerous, difficult, and underpaid job in Pardee's mines, would not be as dangerous to his family if they should stay, if he should remain a poor laborer in these mines.

John, like most of his coworkers, did not speak English, but he believed he knew what it meant to be an American. John foolishly believed the American flag, with all it symbolized and meant to not only him, but to his Anglican superiors, would be enough to defend their cause. Unfortunately this understanding was defeated when he saw the stars and stripes ripped out of the hands of his neighbor, just before he was shot dead. John's understanding of American principles ran away faster than he did, avoiding the gunfire that ripped through the backs of his fleeing cousins and coworkers. Later that night on September 10, 1897, John and his family quickly packed what little belongs they had, and left in the dark, following a winding mountain road that would take them to Eckley, a mining town with little history of violence, a small Polish population, and hopefully employment opportunity. That night when John left the Lattimer mines, he left behind years of unfair labor treatment and social injustice, but more devastatingly, he left behind the American decree he had thought was most important - *liberty and justice for all.*

Peter Gostov, John Breifogel, and Stanley Bierly, Breaker Boys

When Peter, John, and Stanley walked down Main Street from the colliery, they looked like a band of hooligans roughed up from a brawl, and only their laughter and smiles could reveal their boyish frivolity. Knuckles bloodied up as though they scrapped with a rivaling gang, and finger tips missing as if their opponents brought blades to the match, the boys looked intimidating as they walked home down Eckley's dirt road. If one judged the boys only by their appearance, Peter, John, and Stanley would be a menacing group of boys to bump into in the streets. However for their neighbors it was difficult, even laughable, to be afraid of eight and nine year old breaker boys.

By this time of day the sun was starting to sink behind the colliery and the wilderness surrounding Eckley village, and the sun's rays illuminated the coal dust billowing out of the breaker, making the illusion of black snow softly falling and coating the orange, red, and brown leaves still on the trees. This same black dust covered the faces, hands, and clothes of the breaker boys, and the orange sun cast Peter, John, and Stanley as three small blackened imps fixing for a night of mischief, and indeed they were. As they walked past the home of Stanley's Irish neighbor, Peter waved a four fingered hand of hello, and John and Stanley offered an innocent greeting of good evening, yet the frightened face of the old man did not return the same greeting as he hurried back inside his home. Perhaps their neighbor was recalling last October when his outhouse took a walk and positioned itself on the top of his summer kitchen - but what this had to do with the them did not make sense to the breaker boys.

When Stanley entered his kitchen, his mother took his dirty clothes and threw them in a pile by the door, and scrubbed Stanley's hair, face, and hands until his pigment turned from black to red. Quickly changing into cleaner clothes, he rushed out the back door to join an equally scrubbed and red Peter. As they made their way to the street Stanly heard his mother scream – she found the dead snake in his work pants pocket. Before entering John's kitchen a few houses down, Peter and Stanley heard John's father and the other men laughing over their beer and knödels. Inside Peter and Stanley sat next to John at the bottom of the table, and John's father, a big Austrian man with an even bigger laugh, sat at the top next to his oldest son and a few of the other butties he worked with. While the men ate, their conversation turned from joking and laughter, and to talk of the great strike that ended a week earlier. While Johnny Mitch' had secured a victory for the miners and breaker boys, the victory was not without great sacrifice on the part of the miners and their families. Peter, John, and Stanley remembered the past summer and its meager meals, and their fathers watched as their young boys, already forced into maturity working in the breakers, became young men at the ages of eight and nine.

The breaker boys did not grow tired of the potatoes and cabbage their mothers served every night, and graciously rejoiced when their fathers brought home deer and other wild game to supplement for pork, and did not grumble for milk, cheese, or bread. At night when their fathers argued about returning to the mines, the breaker boys stayed up late to listen and learn from them, understanding the magnitude of such decisions. And when Johnny Mitch' came to unite the diverse immigrant work force, Peter the Hungarian, John the Austrian, and Stanley the German understood that ethnic division was the mine's weaponry

to divide them, and the three breaker boys became united strikers and closer friends that summer. The breaker boys Peter, John, and Stanley, though very young in many ways, were hardened by labor and grew up in the summer of 1902, but they had yet to realize it.

Later that evening when the workers returned to their rented homes, John's father realized that Peter, John, and Stanley had not been at the kitchen table for the past hour. Looking down the dark street, he thought he saw three small forms run into the yard of the old Irishman a few houses west, but he could not be sure. The next morning, on the last day of October, Stanley's Irish neighbor woke to use his outhouse, but instead of finding it in its usual place behind his summer kitchen, the old man was horrified to find it in the middle of the street.

Havrilla Vislotsky, Mine Laborer

Havrilla Vislotsky thought Mary Opoletski was a pretty girl, especially when the red and yellow ribbons woven in her wavy blonde hair twisted in the breeze as Mary danced around the young bride with the other maids in the bridal party. Together with the young girls dancing, the children chasing each other, and the married women walking with their bridal boots strung over their shoulders, Havrilla began to think it was time he found himself a wife to take care of him, and that soon it would be his own bridal party walking back to Eckley to celebrate. However Havrilla was also a shy man, and really had only began to think seriously about matrimony during Father's sermon just an hour ago. Havrilla could admire the young girls at Eckley, but only from afar, for he would become too nervous to have a real conversation with them in the store or in his neighbor's kitchens. Havrilla was much more comfortable in the mines, where he knew exactly what was expected of him, and through routine had become very precise in his actions. An interaction with a young woman was much more unpredictable and something he had not practiced very much.

It was popular to make arrangements with coworkers to marry one of their daughters in the old country by financing their voyage to America, and this agreement was tempting for Havrilla – the bride of this wedding arrived this way, and it also involved very little courtship on the part of the bride and groom. Unfortunately, Havrilla's friends teased him, because it did not make sense from him to pay to send for a bride to come over from the old country, when he could pick a Hungarian girl already in Eckley! This method was not only cheaper, but there would be no surprises about the bride's appearance or temperament. Many a man was laughed at when the bride he sent for from his old village not only possessed a hostile temperament, but an earsplitting voice, made worse when she hollered, which would be often. To spare their good friend this embarrassment, Havrilla's coworkers encouraged him to make a good assessment of the young Hungarian women in Eckley, and take advantage of this opportunity to choose wisely, rather than walk blindfolded into a decision about a bride overseas. When it came to choosing the perfect bride, however, Havrilla's friends each had a different opinion. Andrew Klinoski was already married, and after ten years experience, Andrew concluded that a woman who could make a satisfying meal out of left over potatoes, chop firewood when she wasn't picking coal, and required few vanities from the company store would make an ideal wife, and was worth much more than a woman who was pretty but had little durability.

Adolph Minsbor, younger than both Havrilla and Andrew and still a bachelor, believed a little pretty woman was far more important to a man's masculinity than a resourceful, stockier woman, because men who are made little by their wives are not really men at all. Besides, after a few hard years and a couple of children, even a pretty woman becomes hardened and dependable. It was better, Adolph believed, to at least have a woman that for a few years is pretty to look at, than a woman who only goes from bad to worse with time. Even still, the idea of speaking to a young girl, pretty or not, was intimidating to Havrilla, and the anticipation of making arrangements with a girl's father was even more horrifying.

Havrilla's attention turned again to Mary Opoletski, who was still smiling and dancing around the bride. Mary was a very pretty girl, Havrilla thought, but more importantly she did not make him feel foolish in the few occasions when they did speak. Havrilla knew that when her father died in the mines years earlier, she had taken employment as a servant with the Coxe family, so she must know how to take care of a household. Could it be that Havrilla found a woman that was not only pretty and kind to him, but dependable as well – could he have both the women Andrew and Adolph idealized but in the same woman? He would not have to make arrangements with her deceased father, but only get permission from her mother to marry her – and of course, actually talk to Mary much more. Suddenly, Havrilla felt more jovial walking along with the bridal party and became more confident with his matrimonial ambitions. Mary's mother was walking not too far off by herself and Havrilla felt a courageous urge to walk with her, and tell her how much he was looking forward to dancing with her daughter, and how pretty she looked with the red and yellow ribbons in her hair.

1910

The victories of the Strike of 1902 were forgotten throughout the market and labor conflicts during the 1910's, and despite the sacrifices of the thousands of mine laborers during the summer of 1902, what the strike won for them was no longer relevant just over ten years later. By the 1910's, American consumers were beginning to convert to newer and cheaper energies, including bituminous coal, oil, and, by the end of the 1910's, electricity and gas. When anthracite extraction stopped for union representatives to negotiate with employers, the colliery would lose its clientele to alternative energy, whereas in the past consumers did without anthracite, or paid for it at a much higher price during labor strikes and disputes. Once consumers were given energy options, and often cheaper options, negotiations and strikes were no longer effective means for either the miner or the mine owner.

Eckley's population dropped in 1910 to its lowest in fifty years to nine hundred and fifty-two residents. Both Western and Eastern Europeans continued to immigrate to Eckley for work opportunities in the mines and the community, though the Eastern Europeans dominated the workforce at Council Ridge Colliery. And while they sometimes worked together, the Western and Eastern Europeans did not break bread together. The majority of the Eastern Europeans living in Eckley did not worship with the English speaking Catholic congregation in the village, and walked on Sundays to churches in nearby Freeland where they worshipped with a larger community of Catholics who were also from the same cultural backgrounds. By 1910 Eckley's Church of the Immaculate Conception Roman Catholic Church, constructed in the 1860's by Sharpe, Weiss, and Company for its large Irish Catholic population, was seeing fewer pews filled each Sunday, and in just a few more decades the Church would close.

Eventually in 1917 the United States entered World War I, and war manufacturing provided a temporary market boost for anthracite, and Eastern European miners set to work fueling the war machine that was slashing through the country sides and villages of their homelands. War propaganda encouraged miners to mine more coal and remember their first glimpses of freedom shining from Lady Liberty's torch, and encouraged enlistment in Eastern European communities. Imagine the perplexity of a Slavic miner's experience as he enlisted into the United States army to return to the old country to fight against Hungarians and possibly other Slavs, conscripted into service.

For the Slavs and other Eastern Europeans who remained in the mines during World War I, their physical interactions with danger were not very different from the new modern warfare of the Great War in Europe. Loss of limb, death by gas, and bloody explosions could describe casualties in the European trenches as well as in the anthracite mines in northeastern Pennsylvania. Miners belonging to the United Mine Workers union may have gained arbitration rights and better working conditions, but even a successful union arbitration could not negotiate with the earth, and it could not guarantee against mine subsidence, dynamite malfunctions or gas leaks into mine shafts. By the 1910's Sophia Coxe had already constructed a miner's hospital in Drifton near Eckley for the laborers of the Coxe Bros. & Co., but too often casualties of mining accidents were laid across their widow's kitchen table rather than in a hospital bed.

John Bedmer, Miner

In spring 1917 Eckley shook itself dry of the last of winter's snow, the Council Ridge Colliery opened its large mouth by emitting a lazy yawn, and the United States entered World War I. As the miners and laborers who had hibernated throughout the winter stretched their legs to begin work in the mines for another season, the demand for anthracite rose dramatically for war production. Immediately, activity in Council Ridge Colliery exploded and there was no time for a sleepy transition from winter to spring. The mines themselves materialized into a warzone. It was not difficult for a miner to imagine himself in the trenches that gashed through the landscapes of their old villages and homes when like a bomb, the dynamite blasts and the relentless noise deafened their ears, the blinding white flash from the explosion created momentary blindness, while coal dust and earth debris settled in the mouth, eyes, lungs. Allied forces feared mustard gas, and Eckley miners feared white damp. Newly enlisted American soldiers could expect to lose a limb or their lives in Europe, but a miner faced that reality every day, in wartime or peace. As the Hungarian miners in Eckley labored in their own warzone, they wondered about their families and villages in the old country. Were they alive? Conscripted into service against the Allies? Did their villages even exist still, or were they bomb targets? Even before the United States entered the war, Sunday Mass intentions were said for the safety of their families and villages, but by Monday morning these intentions were forgotten as the men entered their own battlefields in the coal mines, and prayers were said for the safe return of husbands and sons from the mines, not from battle.

The men trudged on like soldiers on drill duty into the mines and the women labored in the company homes, protected from any real concerns of the war by their isolation in the mountains of the northern anthracite fields. Only John Bedmer showed any real interest in the war far away in Europe when he and his coworkers walked past the propaganda posters every day, directed especially to the Slavs and Hungarians in Eckley. The first poster showed them a boat full of immigrants pointing and smiling to the Statue of Liberty, 'remember your first thrill of American liberty – buy war bonds!' Very few families in Eckley could afford the extra expense of buying war bonds to support the war, and John's budget certainly could not allow it – with a young bride and infant son, John's family still boarded with a larger family, trying to save enough money to rent their own home. The other poster that struck John on his walk to the mines was a miner standing back to back with an American soldier – 'stand by our boys in the trenches – mine more coal'. John's friends, at least the men who could read English, found this particular propaganda laughable – to them, it was the war and soldiers who were standing by them, making the demand for coal higher, and therefore the demand for miners higher. John however, did not take this poster the same way. Actually, he had a completely different attitude towards the war, his community, and his America.

John Bedmer came to America for many of the same reasons his neighbors and coworkers did. The land his family had farmed for generations was depleted, reaped meager harvests, while the only fertile land was hoarded behind the property lines of overlords. Earning income from dry soil was impossible, so John, along with most of the men in his village, came to Pennsylvania to earn an income from harvesting coal. For ten years John worked in the mines, earning much more money than his family had seen in over a generation, and eventually he saved enough to attract a goodhearted Slovak woman who would give him a son.

All the while John was laboring in the mines, learning to read and write, and earning a respectable income, he was also beginning to define himself. In his old village John was considered a Hungarian, though his family spoke Slovak and identified themselves as Slovak. John could barely read and write Slovak, much less in English, and had no need to learn

28

anymore than was necessary, and after laboring aimlessly in fields that bore him nothing, John struggled to see any worth in himself. John came to the Pennsylvania coal fields and though life here was not a dramatic improvement, there was a noticeable change. When John shoveled his tons of coal, there were no surprises about how much money he would earn, he did not have to wait for months in fruitless anticipation for seeds that would not sprout, for food and earnings that could not be harvested. As a laborer at Council Ridge Colliery, John was taxed and his pay deducted for expenses, but he was always able to save a little aside, and even the little he saved was more than a wasted crop.

John could not understand why the other men did not look at the war with a little more patriotism. For John and the other laborers and miners in Eckley, working in the mines had given them purpose. Working hard had always been in their nature, but as John saw it, at least working in America rewarded them with income and allowed them the potential to rent or own their own homes, and move around for better opportunities. Of course with mining, survival was not a guarantee, and entering old age maimed or crippled in some way was understood, but these physical sacrifices did not come without a lifetime of income. But for John in particular, working in America defined him as a man who worked hard, who earned for his family, who became an American citizen and certified miner. America gave John the ability to see himself as a miner, a man, and a Slavic-American.

The Slavic community in Eckley reprimanded John for enlisting in the United States Army, for breaking away from his community and disrupting the status quo. It was foolish, to leave work in the mines just as the season began, it was foolish, they believed, to sacrifice months of earnings to march about Europe in a war that they hardly understood. To his neighbors, John could 'mine more coal', and still serve his country, but the mines already had hundreds of men to fulfill this duty. No, John wanted desperately to wear the uniform of the United States Army, and to show the Austro-Hungarian Empire that America transformed him from an anonymous peasant to John Bedmer, a miner, a citizen, a soldier of the United States.

By spring 1918, John had served a year of his term, and had wasted away in the European trenches soaked with mud and blood, dying from a leg wound that turned gangrene. On the chilly April morning the Sergeant's letter arrived to bear Mary Bedmer the news she had been widowed, she had been sitting on the front steps of the home she boarded in with her son, Steven, who learned to run just weeks after he learned to walk. A miner who joked at the propaganda John had taken to heart delicately delivered the letter into Mary's hands, left her to read and grieve in peace, and walked the rest of the day to Freeland, to enlist in the United States Army.

Before she could bring herself to open her letter, Mary watched the morning's rays bounce off her son's flaxen blonde hair as he giggled, playing with the dirty laundry his mother had started to scrub before the letter arrived. Mary knew John was dead without having to read the letter, but as she stared at their son, she tried to imagine he could still be alive in Steven. The letter was compassionate and brief, yet poignant, and Mary believed if John could read this letter he would recognize that his service and death was a declaration of his personhood. John had truly believed that America, Eckley, and the mines, had transformed him into a man with purpose, and as his Sergeant wrote, *"an inspiring display of American citizenship and patriotism."*

Mary Katach, Head of Household

Every day when the whistle blew at the colliery to signal the end of the workday in the mines, Mary Katach went out to the front of her house, and patiently watched the men walk down Main Street in Eckley. Mary scanned the blackened faces, looking in a desperate attempt for the familiar features of devilish blue eyes striking out from a black face, and a dusty mustache trimmed carefully above the upper lip. The few men who looked up at Mary standing on her front steps, smiled a sympathetic greeting, and continued down the streets to their wives and rented homes. Mary waited and watched this way every day, more particularly out of habit, because the better part of her knew she would never see her husband walk down from the mines when the breaker whistle blew, for he had not walked down from the mines the past five years. In fact, Mary's husband had not walked anywhere since he was delivered to their home, face draped by another miner's jacket, and laid on the kitchen table. Mary's husband never walked again, but was carried by six of his neighbors to the cemetery in Freeland those five years earlier.

Even though it was a pointless activity, Mary watched the miners walk home every evening, and found comfort from looking at their faces, their alive and structured faces. For as much as she wished she would recognize the face of her departed husband, Mary wished more that she could forget the face, or rather, the devastated flesh, she saw that day when she lifted the miner's jacket from the body of her husband. The men that carried him to their home begged Mary not to lift the jacket, but she could not believe the man lying on her kitchen table was really her husband. The flesh underneath the jacket did not reveal itself at all as the face of Mary's husband, much less the face of anything human – absent were his bright eyes, his lips that were always upturned in a smile, even when he slept, and in their place a gaping mess of blood, flesh, and black powder. It was this sight that Mary saw in her sleep, this sight that she wished to erase by watching the faces of the miners as they walked down Main Street at the end of the workday.

By the time most of the workers had made their way past her home, Mary's oldest sons and her Hungarian boarders had made their way into the kitchen, where she already had wash basins and soap waiting to scrub their faces clean of coal dust and earth. Mary and her nine children had survived the last couple of years and eviction by taking in as many boarders who could fit in the two bedrooms upstairs, and her small half double was never in want of company and noise. To provide even more of an income, when Mary's two oldest boys were of age they were sent to the breaker and the mines, and her heart was in her throat for nine hours a day, and only settled back in her chest when they walked in the kitchen and groaned for supper. At dinner Mary would stare into the faces of her two sons, their skin red from scrubbing them clean, and she could see the face of their father, but slowly their faces would change into the bloody mess, the faceless flesh beneath the miner's jacket that had been the face of her husband – and Mary dreaded that her sons' faces, beautiful and alive, would be ripped apart in the mines by a foolish accident that destroyed their father.

Fortunately, the boyish faces of Mary's sons would never be destroyed in this way, and her oldest son's face would always remain youthful and bright. When the men carried her oldest son down the street and laid him on her kitchen table, his face was just as beautiful and at peace as when he slept, his mangled legs and shredded chest revealed no signs of distress on his face. Mary stared at her son's face for hours, imprinting his image to her memory – and that night when Mary struggled to fall asleep, the butchered face of her husband no longer haunted her, but the rested and complete face of her son chased away her nightmares.

1920

The 1920's was a continuation of failing markets for anthracite in the 1910's, and as the last census decade available for study in Eckley, Pennsylvania, the 1920 census has a foreboding sense of finality for the persons it represents, as they disappear from federal records. After World War I, both domestic and industrial American consumers converted to cheaper energy, and were tired of playing economic games with striking miners and operators withholding anthracite. The number of anthracite coal miners in Pennsylvania dropped dramatically from just the previous decade, as more men became unemployed when collieries bankrupted. Often unemployed miners migrated long distances for jobs outside of the coal fields, or relied on the income of their wives and daughters working in local textile factories. However this shift in gender roles, when the woman became the provider for the family, had detrimental effects on family structure and communities.

The Immigration Act of 1924 put a stop to almost all Eastern European immigration to the United States. Overtime the Eastern European communities and patchtowns in Pennsylvania assimilated themselves into American society, though their affiliation with the Catholic Church and fraternal orders were some of their last connections to the old world traditions that set them apart from their Western European predecessors. Eckley's population rose over one thousand residents again in 1920, despite the failing anthracite market. After the fall of the Austro-Hungarian Empire in World War I, residents in Eckley who previously listed themselves as Hungarian in the 1900 and 1910 census records, were now free to identify themselves as Lithuanian, Beretzkan, Czechoslovakian, Galician, Posenian, Silesian, and Tyrolean. As in the last few decades, the Eastern Europeans in Eckley made up the majority of Council Ridge Colliery's workforce, and many of their Pennsylvanian born children worked in the mines, as well as in the community.

Already by 1920 an elementary school was organized across from the Catholic Church in Eckley, in the east end of the village. Children of both Western and Eastern European immigrants to Eckley realized the value in at least some education, though by adolescence most children were working in the mines or in textile factories in Freeland. However, the official establishment of an elementary school in Eckley did give a few opportunities. The school Americanized the children of immigrants, and encouraged the possibility that some boys might not have to enter the mines as their fathers had. Education raised the possibility that with each new generation, a son became closer to fulfilling the American dream his father had when he left Europe for better opportunities in the anthracite fields. Though an ambitious aspiration, the truth was that in most patchtowns like Eckley, even in 1920, most boys still entered the mines after minimal schooling, and many girls became wives, mothers, and widows within a few short years of each other. In an isolated patchtown such as Eckley, social and economic advancement was often unattainable for immigrant families.

In 1926 Sophia Coxe died at her home in Drifton near the patchtown of Eckley, Pennsylvania, at the dignified age of eighty-five. Aging with grace that only Sophia Coxe could carry beautifully, she left behind generations of mine laborers and their families that had been fortunate enough to work for Eckley B. Coxe, whose hand was continuously guided by his compassionate wife. In the fifty-seven years Sophia Coxe lived in Drifton, surrounded by the patchtowns her husband's collieries created, she tended the wounds, educated, and delighted the poor workforce of Council Ridge Colliery through her benevolent contributions and presence. Eckley lost its father when Richard Sharpe left the community he built in 1874, and in 1926, Eckley's Angel of Anthracite was called back to heaven.

From 1920 on, Eckley's population would continue to decrease as mine operations slowed at the Council Ridge Colliery. Families who once depended on a strong anthracite market left Eckley to work in other industries, or found employment at larger collieries. By the 1960's Eckley's population numbered below five hundred, and strip mining encroached on the village, and destroyed the Jurassic wilderness the Lenape once believed was possessed by evil spirits. As 2010's census would reveal, Eckley's population no longer supported mine operators, miners, laborers, domestics, clergymen, or any of the occupations needed to operate a company-owned town. A single street, Main Street, still exists in Eckley, and the homes constructed by the Sharpe, Weiss, and Company in 1854 still stand on their foundations, though most are empty. Miners are absent from their windows to stare at the snow and coal dust tangle together in the wind. Front steps are neglected by the wives watching for their husbands and sons to return from the mines, and summer kitchens are in want of heat and smoke. The breaker whistle no longer blows from the Council Ridge Colliery, and billows of coal dust and smoke no longer darken the sky or fall on trees and rooftops.

By 1929, just a short seventy-five years had passed in which a few remarkable leaders, dozens of ethnic groups, and thousands of men, women, and children flocked to Eckley in anticipation of job and social opportunities created by the anthracite boom. For seventy-five years, thousands of residents came to Eckley, and by now, they have left the village empty. The history of the labor and social struggles of anthracite communities that defined northeastern Pennsylvania show how so often miners and laborers were just a means to a mine owner's profit. They were objects used and discarded, and left to waste when used up by their company. In a very similar way, the homes left behind by Eckley's miners, laborers, their families and community were means to their own ends. These houses, though company-owned, were temporary tools left behind by their former occupants. Just as the miner was used by his mine operator for profit, these homes were used by the miner, the superintendent, the former slave, the domestic, the clerks, the impoverished, the breaker boys, the widows, and the coal merchant who had come to Pennsylvania's anthracite fields to work, to struggle, to triumph, to perish, to live.

Michael Michlick, Mule Driver

It was still dark in the stables near the Council Ridge Colliery when Sally recognized the approaching footsteps of her mule boy, the Czech Michael Michlick. As Michael came closer into view Sally could make out his gangly silhouette, and she whinnied with excitement she reserved only for Michael when she heard him whistle for her. Michael came to Sally's stall with his usual morning gift of last night's cabbage, and Sally nudged Michaels's chest affectionately as he patted her neck and fussed over her. Attaching her bridle and harness, Michael let Sally affectionately nibble at his hair and his jacket as he led her out of the stables into the misty morning air.

Taking Sally into the mines at Council Ridge Colliery, Michael brought the mule below the earth's surface and hitched Sally to an empty coal car waiting to be led to a mine shaft to be filled with coal and earth. Taking Sally down a shaft, Michael worked with the mine butties loading tons of coal and earth debris into the cars, then walked with Sally out of the shaft to unload their cargo. By the afternoon the miners began working with dynamite to dig deeper into the shaft – and it was not too long before the yellow canaries hanging in their cages began screeching and fluttering furiously with fear. Unknowingly, the miners tapped into a toxic gas pocket, and even with the quick alerts from the canaries, it did not take long for the air left from the explosions to trigger the white damp. A few of the attentive laborers rushed out of the shaft, covering their faces, but the miners closest to the damp had already dropped dead, and only Michael remained desperately trying to pull Sally's reins, who, in alarm, had dug her

33

hooves into the ground, refusing to move. The canaries stopped their screeching and dropped to the bottom of their cages, and Michael, dizzy and weak, leaned onto Sally for support, only to drop to the ground himself, still clutching her halter. Sally's primal senses smelled the death in the mine shaft, and nudged Michael, limp on the ground. Only after recognizing his death, Sally reluctantly left her mule boy in the toxic tunnel. Following her route in the mines, Sally made her way out of the mines on her own and emerged into the light of day, to encounter a crowd of men frantically running about with the breaker whistle blasting in alarm.

The evening following Sally's escape from the mines, a man she had never seen before came to the stables looking nervous, and asked a mule boy how many mules had been lost that day in the mine gas leak. When the mule boy replied that none of the mules had died and made their way out of the mines on their own, the stranger chuckled a sigh of relief. Before leaving the stables, the stranger looked at Sally the way she looked at a stack of timothy hay, and commented that sending expensive property in the mines everyday was a financial risk to the business. The uneasiness Sally had felt went away as soon as the stranger was out of sight, and the mule boy continued to stare in the man's direction as he said to Sally, "funny, he didn't ask me how many mule *boys* were lost today.."

Nellie O'Donnell, Teacher

As Nellie O'Donnell watched the boys and girls run out of her classroom to return home, she wondered why she bothered teaching them poetry and geography when in just a few short years the boys would tend mine doors, sit alone in the dark for ten hours a day, and the girls would be walking to the textile factory in Freeland, or already young mothers. They were still impressionable children, but by the time Nellie's students turn fourteen and fifteen, they would hardly be concerned that there are pyramids in Egypt or a Great Wall in China. Their primary concerns would be how to make their rent and how to keep a family fed throughout the winter when the mines were closed. When her boys and girls reach her age, in their early twenties, they would not remember Richmond's rally, *"true hope is swift, and flies with swallow's wing, Kings it makes gods, and meaner creatures kings"* from Shakespeare's *Richard III*, but they will be able to read an eviction notice. Nellie thinks she'd do better to show her girls how to make five different meals from Sunday's leftover potatoes and teach her boys to manage a budget than to read Thomas More's *Utopia* aloud to them every day.

"Be not afraid of greatness: some are born great, some achieve greatness, and some have greatness thrust upon 'em," – Shakespeare again. Nellie's favorite poster brightens her simple classroom with Malvolio's verse written onto a dirt road as colonial patriots march to make battle with the red coats, America leading them forward, sword drawn and the American flag draped across her body. The line and image is timeless, but the poster itself was yellowed with age, older than Nellie. She first saw it hanging on the wall of the community center in Drifton, Cross Creek Hall, for a Fourth of July celebration thrown by Sophia Coxe when Nellie was nine years old. It was raining on the day of the celebration, so everyone picnicked inside and the children ran about with Uncle Sam masks on while Nellie stayed quietly by her mother's side with the gossiping older women. Nellie noticed the poster, and stared at Malvolio's line, reading the words without really reading the line, her little frame dwarfed by America and the steadfast patriots. When the frail, yet elegant, figure appeared at Nellie's side, she hardly noticed until Sophia Coxe asked Nellie why she preferred to stare at a poster than join the children in games, and could she read this poster? Nellie told Sophia Coxe that she could read the line on the poster, and Nellie had wondered if it was written by an American patriot, to which Mrs. Coxe corrected her that this line was from a

Shakespearean comedy, a playwright the poor daughter of Irish parents had never heard of. Nellie remembered the way Sophia Coxe looked down at her in front of that poster, a yearning look of pity, for Sophia Coxe knowingly imagined that Nellie would someday work in a textile factory, become a young mother and an old woman within a few short years of each other, and this line from *Twelfth Night* would mean nothing to the woman who on this Fourth of July stared intently at this poster, wanting more to learn about Shakespeare than play games with other children.

Sophia Coxe took down the patriotic poster with the borrowed Shakespearean and let Nellie take it home with her that day, and within a week a Webster's *Dictionary* and a collection of Shakespearean plays arrived at Nellie's door, with a note bookmarked in *Twelfth Night,* on top of Malvolio's line. Over the next couple of years Sophia Coxe continued to have plays, poetry, American novels, books on geography, books on botany, and more sent to Nellie, so that over time Nellie grew into a self-educated young woman, compared to the girls who only learned to manage a home and husband. It was Sophia Coxe who set Nellie up at the new school in Eckley next to Drifton, and as a gift of congratulations gave Nellie her personal copy of More's *Utopia*, hoping she could inspire her students with More the way she had been moved by Shakespeare over ten years ago.

But after five years of teaching children who eventually leave her class to become factory girls and black faced boys, Nellie struggled to see the purpose in her profession. Of course she worked as a teacher to have a source of income, to pay the woman she boarded with, and to provide for her parents, but Nellie hoped to see in her students the eagerness she had recognized in herself to read, learn, and become something different than what her mother and father had been. Nellie was beginning to realize how impractical her ambition was because not every child in Eckley could become a teacher when they were depended upon to help support their large families as soon as their bodies were able. Even more realistically, Eckley provided little opportunity for scholars, botanists, and poets – there were only the colliery jobs in the mines and factory jobs in Freeland that promised wages in this isolated community. Nellie wondered why she had made the Hungarian boy memorize poetry, when she attended his funeral a year later, and offered her condolences to a mother grieving the loss of her youngest son in the mines. Why did she assign the quiet Italian girl *Leaves of Grass* when she was married and pregnant within six months? How could *I Sing the Body Electric* have prepared this girl to become a mother? The truth was that Walt Whitman taught her girls nothing about becoming a wife and mother, and poetry did not save the little boys from perishing in the mines. Coming to Nellie's classroom was just a way to bide time between chores, finding a job, or finding a husband in Eckley.

The breaker whistle blew, signaling the end of the workday at Council Ridge Colliery, and after watching the last of her students make their way into their homes, Nellie turned back into her classroom, wondering if her reading today from *Utopia* had struck any of the students in her class. Probably not, as usually the boys and girls looked anywhere but at her as she read from More, mostly because half of her students still spoke their parents' Hungarian or Slovak, and the other half were too preoccupied just being children. Nellie was surprised then to see Joseph Bradish still at his seat, staring at the poster given to her by Sophia Coxe so many years earlier. Joseph's parents were Czech, and the boy struggled with his English, but he was one of the few children who seemed to pay attention to Nellie as she taught and read aloud to the class.

Joseph's face showed that he was struggling with something, and when Nellie sat down next to him, he asked her in his poor English if he understood More correctly. Joseph always came across as shy to Nellie, but perhaps his struggle with English kept him quiet, and he seemed so taken with More's passage today, so eager to understand it, that Nellie assigned Joseph to copy and recite the passage fifteen times – not as a punishment, but to help him improve his English and understand More's message. As Nelllie watched Joseph leave her classroom, she smiled and felt giddy inside, and when she walked down the street her step was lighter. Nellie almost felt as though she was skipping home, just happy that this little boy took an interest in her readings.

That night after supper, Joseph Bradish sat down at the dinner table, and slowly copied his assigned line from *Utopia* fifteen times. After each time he finished a line, Joseph stared at it, contemplated its meaning, and compared it to English and Czech phrases he knew until he believed he came to a conclusion. Joseph readied himself for bed, never before so excited to go to Miss O'Donnell's class the next morning, to ask his teacher if he understood More correctly. Before he slipped into bed, Joseph took one last look at the line, and spoke it out loud to himself – *"What you cannot turn to good, you must at least make as little bad as you can"*.

Epilogue

Before I worked through the census records on site at Eckley Miners' Village, Pennsylvania, the names in *Patchtown* had not been seen, heard, or spoken of since the last persons who knew them said their names aloud. Until now, no one knew that Catherine Given, by the age of eighteen, was already living and working in Eckley on her own. Few probably knew that James Mason, his wife and their seven children were the first and only African American family to pass through Eckley, and took their chances at industrial slavery to work in the mines and raise a family away from Southern slavery. While we have general understandings of who lived in Eckley between 1860 and 1920, Eckley's individuals have been neglected and their personal stories have been forgotten.

Eckley is a representation of an anthracite patchtown from the nineteenth and twentieth centuries, but in many ways, Eckley is exceptional, due largely in part by the individuals who came to Eckley, and their own unique circumstances. The most harm that could be inflicted on Eckley would be to generalize this patchtown and its residents. To present Eckley, its demographics, its social make-up, and its history as a cookie cutter image of an anthracite patchtown would be a great misconception and a discredit to its former occupants. To understand Eckley accurately and personally, one need only to spend a few hours exploring the village's census records. One of the census record's many surprises begins in the 1860's. Despite the generalizations of local history, Eckley's Irish workforce supported more superintendents and engineers than Eckley's English and Welsh population in the 1860's through the 1880's. Eckley might have been Paramount Picture's backdrop for *The Molly Maguires*, but Eckley's history did not provide the script nor the characters for the 1968 film. Though *The Molly Maguires*, Sean Connery and Richard Harris popularized local Irish labor history and used Eckley as their setting, they also overshadowed the stories of men and women like John Nogal, Mary Katach, and Michael Michlick. Over the course of the village's sixty recorded years in the census records, Eckley's population represented twenty different nationalities, whose residents came mostly from Eastern European countries. Local nostalgia of *The Molly Maguire* film and popular culture's glamorization of this captivating secret society overlooks the individuals of Eckley's other nineteen nationalities.

Historical generalizations are really historical stereotyping. For Eckley in particular, the Irish had a slightly different experience than the Irish in other patchtowns and communities, and over the course of seventy-five years, the Irish were not the only group of men and women to live, die, work, and struggle in Eckley. If *Patchtown* accomplished anything, it shed new light on Eckley, and resurrected a few of the persons who could help to clarify this patchtown's unique history. The worst that could happen to the thousands of residents in Eckley's census records would to be mistreated by historical interpretation. By giving voice to these forgotten men, women, and children of Eckley's past, their lives and histories will no longer be ignored.

Bibliography

"110 Years Ago." Standard Speaker [Hazleton, PA] 1 Feb. 2011. Print.

"110 Years Ago." Standard Speaker [Hazleton, PA] 11 Dec. 2010. Print.

"110 Years Ago." Standard Speaker [Hazleton, PA] 15 Feb. 2011. Print.

"110 Years Ago." Standard Speaker [Hazleton, PA] 17 Mar. 2011. Print.

"110 Years Ago." Standard Speaker [Hazleton, PA] 2 Dec. 2010. Print.

"110 Years Ago." Standard Speaker [Hazleton, PA] 23 Mar. 2011. Print.

"110 Years Ago." Standard Speaker [Hazleton, PA] 24 Dec. 2010. Print.

"110 Years Ago." Standard Speaker [Hazleton, PA] 27 Nov. 2010. Print.

"110 Years Ago." Standard Speaker [Hazleton, PA] 27 Sept. 2010. Print.

"110 Years Ago." Standard Speaker [Hazleton, PA] 28 Sept. 2010. Print.

"110 Years Ago." Standard Speaker [Hazleton, PA] 30 Oct. 2010. Print.

"110 Years Ago." Standard Speaker [Hazleton, PA] 4 Apr. 2011. Print.

"110 Years Ago." Standard Speaker [Hazleton, PA] 5 Mar. 2011. Print.

"110 Years Ago." Standard Speaker [Hazleton, PA] 7 Oct. 2010. Print.

Aurand, Harold, and William Gudelunas. "The Mythical Qualities of Molly Maguire."
    Pennsylvania History 49 (1982): 91-105. *JSTOR.* Web. 6 Oct. 2010.

Bohning, James L. "Angel of the Anthracite: The Philanthropic Legacy of Sophia Georgina
    Coxe." *Canal History and Technology Proceedings* 24 (2005): 150-82. *JSTOR.* Web. 2
    Oct. 2010.

Da Costa Nunes, Jadviga M. "Pennsylvania's Anthracite Mines and Miners: A Portrait of the
    Industry in America Art, C. 1860-1940." *The Journal of the Society for Industrial
    Archeology* 28 (2002): 11-32. *JSTOR.* Web. 12 Sept. 2010.

Dublin, Thomas, and Walter Licht. "Gender and Economic Decline: The Pennsylvania
    Anthracite Region, 1920-1970." *The Oral History Review* 27 (2000): 81-97. *JSTOR.*
    Web. 15 Oct. 2010.

Glass, Brent D. "Massacre at Lattimer, An American Rite of Passage: An Interview with
    Michael Novak." *Pennsylvania Heritage* 23 (1997): 4-13. *JSTOR.* Web. 8 Sept. 2010.

Kenny, Kevin. "The Molly Maguires and the Catholic Church." *Labor History* 36 (1995): 345-76. *JSTOR*. Web. 26 Sept. 2010.

Kenny, Kevin. "The Molly Maguires in Popular Culture." *Journal of American Ethnic History* 14 (1995): 27-46. *JSTOR*. Web. 29 Sept. 2010.

Korson, George. "Anthracite Miners as Bards and Minstrels." *American Speech* 10 (1935): 260-68. *JSTOR*. Web. 4 Oct. 2010.

Landis, Mary Ann. "Labor and Coal: The Beginnings of a Regional Union in the Anthracite Fields of Pennsylvania, 1854-1874 - Part I." *The Chronicle of the Early American Industries Association, Inc* 52 (1999): 114-21. *JSTOR*. Web. 29 Sept. 2010.

Lauver, Fred J. "Visiting the Museum of Anthracite Mining: A Walk Through the Rise and Fall of Anthracite Might." *Pennsylvania Heritage* 27 (2001): 32-39. *JSTOR*. Web. 22 Sept. 2010.

Maxey, Hucie. "Lillybrook, the Memories Never Die." *Goldenseal* 34.3 (2008): 53-57. *JSTOR*. Web. 8 Oct. 2010.

Miller, Donald L., and Richard E. Sharpless. *The Kingdom of Coal: Work, Enterprise, and Ethnic Communities in the Mine Fields*. Philadelphia: University of Pennsylvania, 1993. Print.

Noon, Mark A. "Martin Ritt Takes on the Molly Maguires." *Pennsylvania Heritage* 27 (2001): 12-21. *JSTOR*. Web. 8 Oct. 2010.

US Census Bureau. 1860. Eckley Miners' Village, Eckley, Pennsylvania.

US Census Bureau. 1870. Eckley Miners' Village, Eckley, Pennsylvania.

US Census Bureau. 1880. Eckley Miners' Village, Eckley, Pennsylvania.

US Census Bureau. 1900. Eckley Miners' Village, Eckley, Pennsylvania.

US Census Bureau. 1910. Eckley Miners' Village, Eckley, Pennsylvania.

US Census Bureau. 1920. Eckley Miners' Village, Eckley, Pennsylvania.

Made in the USA
Charleston, SC
04 November 2011